QUEEN VICTORIA

Empress of India

THE HISTORY HOUR

HISTORY

CONTENTS

❧ I ❧
INTRODUCTION

❦

Look back in time as you visit the life of one of the most powerful women in the world when she turned eighteen years old. Queen Victoria may have been a lonely child, but she was thrown into the spotlight before dawn one morning when her uncle passed away.

❦

She enjoyed what was considered the most luxurious trappings and furnishings of her time. Compared to the way we live today, some of their ways of living would still seem archaic at best.

❦

There were no phones, no airplanes, no cars, no running water, no microwaves, no indoor toilets, no ice makers, no easy way to take a bath and for certain no showers. There were plenty of servants for the rich.

❧

To visit friends, you had to ride in a carriage, and in the winter, there was no heating in that carriage, so it was cold inside your ride.

❧

For Queen Victoria you will find she lived life large. She loved deeply and mourned deeper. Her love for her Albert never left her to the day she died.

❧

Many rumors abound that there were other lovers and that she was drawn to many men. Some proven, some not.

❧ II ❧

THE BIRTH THAT ALTERED WORLD HISTORY

"Great events make me quiet and calm; it is only trifles that irritate my nerves."

— QUEEN VICTORIA

❦

It was like any other day to most people living in the United Kingdom, but this was not to be the instance May 24th, 1819 at Kensington Palace. This day, believe it, or not, would alter the course of history for years to come, and no one would realize it for seventeen years.

❦

Victoria's father, the Duke of Kent, rejected his mistress he had been with for many years and married widow Victoire, the Duchess of Amorbach. When the Duchess was found to be pregnant, it was duly noted so as soon as she could travel, they had to leave her German country and make sure she gave birth to their child on good old English soil so that there would be no question about her possible inheritance to the throne of England.

⚜

The Duke was so plagued with debt that had been unresolved by the sovereign, that he had run into delay after delay to raise enough money to be able to bring his wife and all their belongings across the English Channel. The Duchess was all the way into her eighth month before they could sail and did not arrive at Dover until April 24th; barely a month before the baby was to be born. At Kensington Palace, the Monarch, the Duke's brother, allowed them to live in an apartment, but he was not happy that his brother was there because he was so wasteful.

⚜

She was christened as Alexandrina Victoria Hanover in a private ceremony June 24th, 1819 at Kensington Palace in the Cupola Room. The name Alexandrina came from one of her godparents who was the Emperor of Russia; Alexander I. Victoria was for her mother. She was born to Princess Victoria of Saxe-Coburg-Saalfeld and Prince Edward, the Duke of Strathearn and Kent who held the position as the fourth son of King George the III of the United Kingdom. Alexandrina Victoria Hanover would be their only child.

⚜

There had been other names proposed for this new precious child, some of which were Charlotte, Georgiana, and Augusta, but they were all discounted by Baby Victoria's Uncle George, the Prince Regent.

꧁꧂

The birthing of a Royal in that era was not a fun process. It was usually painful, lasted forever, and everyone that was anyone it seemed was present in the room for the complete process. Yes, that is what I said, you read right, everyone was there to watch you suffer and scream as there were no pain relievers to give, that would not harm the newborn, and the onlookers were there so they could encourage the pregnant woman who was in labor, and to be able to swear that no foul play had taken place if the baby born should happen to die.

꧁꧂

If a child could be an heir to the British throne, it would require witnesses to be present in the room to watch the birth as it was happening. The room was so crowded with midwives, doctors, servants, ladies in waiting, and male courtiers.

꧁꧂

There were always worries that there might be a crooked monarch that would try to replace a baby born dead with a different male newborn. They would sneak the different baby in with a warming pan. Later, after the Reformation, you would find that Protestants worried that the Catholic Stuarts might try to cheat and divert the heir to the throne away from Protestant Hanoverians.

❧❧❧

In 1894, Queen Victoria put a stop to this practice and said that they only needed the home secretary present.

❧❧❧

As Victoria was growing up in Kensington Palace, she led a quiet if not secluded life with her mother and the servants. Her mother was of German descent, so she taught Victoria German as her first language.

❧❧❧

Never expecting to be Queen of anything, she learned to speak English fluently. Her mother did ensure that Victoria was educated in history, natural philosophy, foreign languages, drawing, and music.

❧❧❧

When Victoria was still a child, she was fun-loving, warm-hearted, lively, and a little mischievous. She was naturally graceful and carried herself with poise.

❧❧❧

At the time Victoria was born she was fifth in line to the throne should anything happen to the four oldest sons of George the 3rd. Victoria was the daughter of the youngest of the sons to inherit the throne, the Duke of Kent.

❧❧❧

In 1820, Victoria's grandfather and Victoria's father "***both***" died in the very same week. Over the next ten years, everyone ahead of her for the throne with the exception of George the 3rd son William had died. George the 3rd's son William had two daughters, but they had died as infants, and it forced William to name his niece Victoria as the heir to the throne and of what was seen then as a growing British Empire.

❧

Victoria was only eleven when it was realized she would be the heir to the King who was aging. King George IV died in 1830, and it was a certainty Victoria would be a part of British politics, and by the time she turned thirteen, she would be the heir to the throne. Victoria's life was miserable because now she had been thrown into the spotlight and her Mother who had always been controlling was even more so now. Sir John Conroy, a man Victoria hated with all her being, pushed her Mother to be even more controlling as well. Rumor had it John Conroy was her mother's accountant and her lover. He had been her father's assistant before he died.

❧

It was when she was thirteen that John Conroy started organizing what was "***semi-royal***" tours so that Princess Victoria was out and about being "***introduced***" to her countrymen and the nation. Everyone welcomed Victoria.

❧

Conroy was working to dominate Victoria, the future Queen of Britain. He persuaded Victoria's mother that they must protect Victoria from her "***wicked uncles***," because they were a threat, so the Duchess started using the "**Kensington System**" to rear Victoria. By this system, Victoria was isolated from her friends and her father's relatives. Conroy was trying to make Victoria dependent only on himself and to one day use his power to reign over the monarchy.

❦

Conroy had not anticipated such a strong-willed young woman who was supported by Lehzen, her governess.

❦

There is a story, (this author is not claiming it as truth, but from the source it came, it does make one wonder) found written in the many volumes of Queen Victoria's diaries that tell of the young Princess Victoria at age 15 who entertained a secret affair with one Scottish Earl – Lord Elphinstone, who was twelve years older than Victoria.

❦

During that time, it was nothing for a royal or a Lord to come to Europe and settle there, snatch a pretty 14-year-old young lady from a nobleman's house and marry her. It happened all the time, and no one thought anything about it. In our time it is quickly labeled pedophilia.

❦

More than a decade later, Victoria would make sure that Lord Elphinstone was brought back to her Royal household in a higher position than he had been in his previous stay. He would now be a Lord-in-Waiting. The year, 1847.

＊＊＊

How in the world she could sneak out from her mother and John Conroy's eyesight is a miracle in and of itself? One must wonder how they met, where they met and how the clandestine affair was carried out. Being Captain of the Horse Guard was an easy way for them to have met. I suppose; but from there, how she could keep sneaking out of the house without suspicion is so beyond this writer.

＊＊＊

If the affair (out-of-wedlock) at that, between Lord Elphinstone and Victoria, did produce a girl child and it was ever found out publicly, it would have torn down the reign of Victoria and the entire house of Windsor.

＊＊＊

The intense fear that the relationship would be found out was so terrible that Elphinstone was quickly exiled to India, to be the governor of the capital city Madras.

＊＊＊

The Royal generations since have kept Victoria's secret, which of course had been written by Queen Victoria and all her letters to her first-born child "*Vicky*," who when she turned 17 was bound in an arranged marriage with a Prussian Prince and after all that had happened was to become Queen Victoria's greatest confidante.

＊＊＊

It was in 1835 when sniveling John Conroy tried his best to persuade young Victoria to sign paperwork that would extend her minority. It stated that she would not be able to gain the throne until she was 25 instead of 18 years old. He felt if he could do this and William the 4th died before Victoria turned 25, then the Duchess, who Conroy had control over, would be made the Regent and he would have control of the Monarchy.

❦

What was even worse, John Conroy and Victoria's mother decided to try and seize her powers. After Victoria had returned from an extended tour, she developed what was diagnosed then as typhoid fever. Victoria was so ill for five weeks that she could not even walk. She lay in her bed, so weak and her hair falling out by the clumps, begging that someone call for a doctor.

❦

It did not matter; her mother nor Conroy were not about to bring in a doctor.

❦

Conroy went so far as to hold Victoria's hand with the pen in it over where she needed to sign the paperwork to let him be her treasurer and adviser. That would give John Conroy total power over all of Victoria's affairs until she turned 25.

❦

Conroy became angry, and he and Victoria's mother threatened to starve her and lock her up if she did not sign those papers. Victoria, as sick as she was, was smarter than he had planned and did not give in and would not sign the paperwork.

ᘓᣟᘐ

It was Victoria's governess, Miss Louise Lehzen who couldn't stand it any longer who secretly called the doctor and got some help for Victoria. It was true that Victoria almost died, but she did not sign the papers.

ᘓᣟᘐ

In the diary she kept every day, she wrote,

> *"in spite of how ill I was and how horrible they were,*
> *I resisted."*

ᘓᣟᘐ

She was never allowed to have her own bedroom until she became Queen. She could not walk up or down the stairs unless an adult was holding on to her hand. Most surprising is that she came out of all of this mentally unscathed, or not, you decide. With what she had been going through, she should have been a nervous wreck.

❧ III ❧
NOW THE THRONE

"The important thing is not what they think of me, but what I think of them."

— QUEEN VICTORIA

❦

The Lord Chamberlain and Archbishop of Canterbury came to Kensington Castle in the wee hours of June 20th, 1837 to let Princess Victoria know that her uncle King William the IV had died.

❦

That morning the Privy Council seemed impressed that the young queen was found to be so assured and graceful in her demeanor. Even though she was tiny in frame, she carried herself elegantly, and her voice was so soft to whomever she spoke. It would be a voice that she kept her entire life.

※

Since Victoria had never had a room of her own and to herself, she exiled her mother immediately to a group of apartments at the other end of Buckingham Palace.

※

The second thing she made sure happened was that John Conroy was no longer an employee of the castle. She also made sure that her uncle Leopold got a stern warning that he could not be discussing the politics of the British out in public.

※

One thing about becoming Queen when Victoria looked back on her life; she found to be the most satisfactory period of her service was due to her friendship and infatuation with Prime Minister, Lord Melbourne.

※

Part of Victoria seemed to be in love with Melbourne, and maybe he with her. But Melbourne had been through a lot. His wife had had a very public affair with Lord Byron, and Melbourne's only child had died. He was sad in many ways, but he spent five to six hours a day with Victoria and seemed to enjoy their time together.

※

Melbourne had a strong influence with Victoria, and he educated her extensively on the government that she oversaw. Melbourne was a sophisticated man, and he helped the new queen with her enthusiasm and self-confidence in her new role; he told her to ignore and try to minimize all those social problems she would encounter and remember that all the unrest and discontented people were just agitators. Melbourne was the reason that Victoria became a very staunch Whig.

༄༅

Because Victoria was constitutionally partisan, it caused or at least contributed to the first of two crises she would deal with as Queen that began in 1839.

༄༅

One was with Lady Flora Hastings who was allied and connected with the Tories, also a maid of honor, who Victoria forced that she be examined by a doctor to see if she was pregnant because of her large abdomen.

༄༅

When it was found that Victoria was wrong, the gossip picked up speed and became damaging for Victoria and much worse when later that same year, poor Lady Flora, died from liver cancer in the advanced stages that the doctor had found when he had examined her for a possible pregnancy.

❧ IV ❧

THE PEOPLE'S ENTHUSIASM ABOUT THE CORONATION WAS QUICKLY DISSIPATING

❀

Then there was the famous "***bedchamber crisis***." When Lord Melbourne resigned, a Sir Robert Peel who was a Conservative leader, said that the ladies of the bedchamber who were Whigs should be taken out.

❀

Queen Victoria said that would not be happening unless Lord Melbourne said it was a good idea. She wanted them all to know that she was not falling for their tricks just because she was a woman.

❀

Sir Robert Peel refused to take the office of Prime Minister, so Lord Melbourne came back to it, not really wanting to, but did nevertheless.

❦

The day assigned for Queen Victoria's coronation was June 28th, 1838. England was ready for the festivities. There were 400,000 of affectionate and delighted subjects that lined the streets as the Queen's procession passed by; even though it was early morning, London seemed so alive, and a long time before the parade was to start, people were everywhere getting their places for a good view.

❦

At precisely 10:00 a.m., the Queen's procession started up Constitution Hill after leaving the Palace. The Queen could see from the Hill all the preparations being made for the fair that was going to be held at Hyde Park.

❦

The parade passed Piccadilly, bells were ringing, people were rejoicing, and they all seemed genuinely delighted. The procession then turned onto St. Jame's Street and then Pall Mall where club-houses and balconies were full of ladies dressed in their finest, while others were waving handkerchiefs and cheering.

❦

They then turned on Parliament Street heading for the Abbey, where the platforms were covered with people. The Peeresses and the Peers, dressed in their robes of estate, and others who had been asked to attend the ceremony were already seated in the Abbey before the Queen arrived.

☙❧

Once at the Abbey, Queen Victoria was greeted by her Officers of State, the Bishops carrying the Patina, the Nobleman bearing the Regalia, the Bible, the Chalice, when Victoria went to her robing chamber to the right of the coronation platform.

☙❧

There in front of the grand western entrance of the Abbey, there was an impressive Gothic structure with the style of the architecture fitting perfectly with the aged Abbey itself. To the left and the right of this porch were reception rooms for Victoria and members of her Royal Family. Beautifully carved oak doors opened into the chambers. The right chamber was for the Queen and was entered by an anti-chamber, where her ladies would remain.

☙❧

Over the Naïve (unstructured) floor they had placed a beautiful floor, and over the aisles on the sides, there had been galleries made to hold 1,500 people. The galleries were designed to hold theater arranged seats that had been covered with a red cloth. The fronts of the seats were decorated with red drapery and some gold trim; canvass screens draped from the bottom of the galleries all the way to the floors. The floors being painted an imitation masonry.

☙❧

Looking in the direction of where the choir was seated in the theatre, there was a gorgeous Gothic screen, which covered the organ loft and the gallery for the musicians. To the average eye, it looked like solid masonry. Under this screen was support for the music gallery, and a succession of Gothic pillars, that formed a type of vestibule, and this is where the procession passed through.

꧁꧂

The theatre of the Abby was where the magnificent decorations filled one's mind with astonishment. At the front where the altar stood in its Gothic canopy and with its beautiful lattice, the place where all significant ceremonies always took place; even nearer than that was the platform where the chair sat that the Queen would receive the homage from the Peers.

꧁꧂

Above the altar where the gallery was for the reception of members of the House of Commons; and higher above this there was another gallery that was added that displayed the Queen's arms which were beautifully decorated.

꧁꧂

You could see on the left and right in the high altitude, galleries to hold people who had bought tickets for this great moment. In the choir area, there were extra seats that were also decorated with gilt Gothic panels and the lower section of the chairs being made from wainscoting.

꧁꧂

When Queen Victoria ascended the theatre and passed to the south side of the Royal Throne, she went to her Chair of State which was the Recognition Chair. She proceeded to have her private devotion as she kneeled at her footstool, and then she took her seat; her supporters and the Bishops who were on either side of her standing with the Noblemen who were wearing the symbolic Four Swords stood at her right hand, and the Royal Person was the nearest to the Sword of State.

༄

The Lord High Constable and the Lord Great Chamberlain stood to Victoria's left. The Noblemen who were bearing the Regalia, the Great Officers of State, Deputy Garter, Dean of Westminster, and Black Rod, were all standing by the chair of Victoria; the Bishops were holding the Bible, the Patina, and the Chalice as they stood near the pulpit. Lord Chamberlain of the Household, Groom of the Robes, and the Train-bearers were all standing behind Victoria.

༄

After the Anthem was finished, Archbishop of Canterbury stepped forward from his place, and with Lord Chancellor, the Lord High Constable, the Lord Great Chamberlain, Deputy Garter, and Earl Marshal all moved to the east of the theatre where Archbishop made Recognition. The trumpets were sounding, and the drums were being beaten. Victoria then sat back down. The Officers of the Wardrobe spread out a cloth of gold, laid on it a cushion so Victoria could kneel on the pillow, at the steps leading to the altar where the Archbishop of Canterbury walked towards the altar and put on his cape.

Victoria was then accompanied by her supporters, to the altar. There Victoria kneeled on the same cushion and placed her first offering which was a pail of gold altar cloth. Treasurer of the household then presented a bar of gold, that weighed a pound, to Lord Great Chamberlain who in turn gave it to Victoria and she then gave it to the Archbishop who placed it in the offering basin. After another prayer, Victoria stood up and walked back just as before with her attendants to her Chair of State.

A sermon was given and once concluded, Archbishop of Canterbury, moved towards Victoria and stood in front of her. He asked her the questions required of the incoming Royalty, which she answered, Victoria stood up, and again attended by Lord Great Chamberlain and her supporters – the sword of state was brought before Victoria. She went to the altar where she knelt down on her cushion and placed her right hand on the "***Holy Gospels***," given to Victoria per the Archbishop. Victoria took the Oath of Coronation, then kissed the book of Gospels, and on a copy of the oath signed her Royal signature.

Lord Chamberlain of the Household had been delivered by an officer of the Jewel Office a silver pen just for that purpose. As Victoria returned to her chair, the choir sang a hymn and the Archbishop read the first line of the song, "***Come Holy Ghost, our Souls inspire***."

At the end of the song, the Archbishop read a prayer that was preparing for the anointing. At the end of the anthem Victoria stood up from her chair, went to the altar, and her crimson robe was removed. Victoria then walked over and sat in St. Edward's chair which was covered in gold, with a footstool in front of it when she was anointed; four Knights of the Garter held over Victoria's head cloth of gold. The Dean of Westminster took the ampule of consecrated oil from the altar and poured some of it into an anointing spoon. Victoria was then anointed on her hands and head in the form of the cross and chanting, "**_Be thou anointed_**." When this part was over, Victoria resumed sitting in St. Edward's chair.

The Dean then took the spurs away from the altar and took them to Lord Great Chamberlain, who then knelt down and presented them to Victoria, who returned them to be laid on the altar. Viscount Melbourne, who was carrying the sword of state, took it back to Lord Chamberlain got another sword that was in a sheath made of purple velvet, which was redelivered by his Lordship to the Archbishop who then laid it on the altar and prayed. The sword was then removed from the altar by the Archbishop and with several other Archbishops took the sword to the Queen and lay it in her right hand. Victoria then took the sword in the holder and gave it to the Archbishop who placed it on the altar.

Victoria while standing, was dressed in the Royal robe of gold cloth and then she sat down. The Archbishop took an orb from the Dean, placed in on Victoria's right hand. Victoria gave it back to the Dean, who then set it on the altar as well.

Lord Chamberlain of Victoria's Household received a ruby ring from the officer from the Jewel Office. It was brought to the Archbishop who placed it on Victoria's fourth finger on her right hand asking her to receive the ring.

It was the Dean then that brought the scepter from the altar along with the cross, the scepter with a dove, and gave them to the Archbishop. While this was taking place, the Duke of Norfolk, who was Lord of Manor Workshop, left his seat, approached Victoria, kneeled, and gave her a glove to wear on her right hand, that was embroidered with the Howard arms which Victoria put on. Then the Archbishop took the Scepter and the Cross and put it in Victoria's right hand and the Dove and Scepter in her left side saying,

"Receive the Rod of Equity."

Victoria stepped up into the theatre and to help her to get on her throne was Bishops, Archbishops, and Peers surrounding her. Once upon the throne, everyone was standing around the steps of the Throne the Archbishop said,

"Stand firm and hold fast."

It was the Archbishop who knelt before Victoria and pronounced all the words of Homage and as all the officials kneeled around and repeated after him. The Archbishop kissed Victoria's hand, and everyone else did the same and left. There was a succession of Dukes, illustrious uncles, and various other officials who all came by and touched Victoria's crown and then kissed her left cheek or hand and then left as the choir sang.

❦

The Bishops of Rochester and Carlisle after the anthem read the Gospel and the Epistle, took from the Altar, the chalice and the patina and carried them into the Chapel of St. Edward's. The bread was brought out on the patina, and the wine was served in the chalice. Victoria took the scepters and gave them the Dukes of Richmond and Norfolk, stepped down from her Throne, accompanied by all her officials walked to the altar and took off her Crown, gave it to the Lord Great Chamberlain for him to hold. She then went to her knees and partook of the sacrament.

❦

The next offering was a purse of gold, was made. Afterward, Victoria got the crown from Lord Great Chamberlain, put it on, and went back to her throne, taking her scepter in her right hand, and the dove scepter in her left. The service was considered concluded, and everyone went into St. Edward's Chapel. Victoria took off her gold robe and put on her Purple Velvet Robe. She then walked out of the choir, through the west door of the Abbey, wearing her beautiful crown, carrying her scepter with the cross in her right hand and her left hand the orb.

The next offering was a purse of gold. Afterward, Victoria received the Crown from Lord Great Chamberlain, put it on, went back to her throne, taking her scepter in her right hand, and the dove scepter in her left hand. The service was considered concluded; everyone went into St. Edward's Chapel. Victoria took off her gold robe and put on her Purple Velvet Robe. She then walked out of the Abbey wearing her beautiful crown, carrying her scepter in her right hand, and in her left the orb.

The procession assembled once more, with Victoria leading the return to Buckingham Palace. The moment Victoria emerged from the Abbey, the crowd went wild shouting with joy which seemed to affect the Queen, who was very tired from everything that she had gone through that day.

The robe that Victoria was dressed in to be crowned was nine yards long (27 feet which must have made it very heavy). There were figures of the crown, the shamrock, the rose and the thistle embroidered on it. The Fleur-de-lis, the eagle, and some other of the different national emblems were shown to be prominent and skillfully made by the manufacturer.

Victoria's under-dress was made of white satin and gold brocade. Her mother wore a dress similar to that but in a different pattern.

The hangings inside the Abbey itself consisted of six hundred yards of purple satin that had been embroidered with silk thread gold flowers.

The document that Victoria signed that day had the name of Alexandrina Victoria on it, but she took the name of "*Alexandrina*" off and told them she only wanted to use Victoria as her name. Her first name after that day was never used again.

On becoming Queen, Victoria realized how little she knew about politics, and Lord Melbourne who was the Whig Prime Minister was leading the government would be the one to work with her. She relied heavily on him for political advice. Victoria made sure she was a financially prudent Queen and worked for paying off all of her father's debts he had left behind.

During her first days as Queen, Victoria's Mother was still living at the palace. It was only by a law that the Duchess of Kent was still there in the palace with her daughter, as it was required until Victoria married, that she must stay with her mother.

Victoria's mother, feeling sure that her days were numbered and fearing for her future, said to Victoria,

"You should forgive me for what displeased you."

⚜

Victoria's mother could forget that. She was married approximately six months after being crowned as Queen. She kicked her mum out of the castle and went so far as to kick her out of town.

⚜

Once Victoria took over the throne, she managed it alone. Because of the way her mother had treated her when she was accompanied by John Conroy, Victoria stayed estranged from her mother, and it caused her caution on any friendships in the future. Victoria had a long memory, and it did not let her forgive anyone easily.

⚜

Victoria rarely spoke to her mother. But, when she started having children, she did allow her mother to visit the palace, but there was no way she and her mother would ever have a typical mother-daughter relationship.

⚜

In 1859, Victoria's mother became extremely ill. It surprised Victoria that it bothered her more than she ever thought that it would. Victoria said,

"I hardly knew who I was and how much I cared about her until I could see looming on the horizon the possibility I cannot mention."

❧

After this illness, her mother recovered, but she became extremely ill again in a couple of years. Her battle with death ended in 1861. Her mother happened to die the same year as Prince Albert.

❧

Victoria started to feel her childhood was closing in on her. She went to her mom's house shortly after her death, and in it, she saw bits and pieces of things from her childhood everywhere.

❧

Victoria always felt her mother hated her. Inside her mother's home was everything from Victoria's childhood. Her mother had kept EVERY pair of shoes that Victoria had ever worn as a baby and every little toy that Victoria had called her own.

❧

Victoria did not realize until then that her mother had in her own way loved her.

WHAT A WEDDING!

"A marriage is no amusement but a solemn act, and generally a sad one."

— QUEEN VICTORIA

Now Prince Albert was the second son, born to the first wife of the Duke reigning over Saxe-Coburg-Saalfeld. When Albert was a young child, he seemed nervous, delicate and had a beautiful face. He was smart, had a good education in science, music, politics, languages, and literature. With this and good morals and physical training as well, he had great wisdom. He had traveled extensively; mostly around Holland, Austria, and Germany to add more to his knowledge.

Rumor and I say this as there are many versions, and it makes it hard to believe with Victoria and Albert having nine children, BUT, Prince Albert was a sensitive and kind of feminine eighteen-year-old VIRGIN when Victoria got her first glance at his gorgeously shaped legs in his sexy pants that were so skin-tight.

❧

It had been suspected that he was a late homosexual bloomer, as when Albert was asked why he had never been among the women and sowed his wild oats he had responded,

"The species of vice is disgusting to me."

❧

Duke of Coburg and two of his sons, Prince Albert and Prince Ernest, visited in the Spring in 1836 during May with the royal family in England. They stayed about a month at Kensington Palace visiting with the Duchess of Kent. They spent their days at Windsor and met members of the royal family while in England. They visited all the famous attractions around the country.

❧

When Prince Albert went back to his home in Coburg, he had a smiling welcome awaiting him from his cousin, a portrait of the young Queen of England. She had sent her portrait and had asked his staff to put it in a spot so that it would be the first thing he saw when he returned home.

❧

In the fall of that year, October to be specific, Albert went back to England for the third time. Victoria was able to shower more affections this time around on her cousin. The dinners she held would sometimes be followed by dances. Of course, Queen Victoria always danced with Albert. There was a time during one of the Castle balls that Victoria gave Albert a bouquet of flowers. Albert was dressed in a uniform that fastened up to the chin and had no buttonholes to hold this bouquet. Albert was brilliant and quick-witted; he took his pocket knife, slit a hole in his jacket and placed the royal bouquet as close to his heart as he could.

◉⚡◉

It did not matter, once Victoria had set her eyes on Albert with his good looks, and her Uncle Leopold kept encouraging her, she proposed to Albert, her cousin October 15th, 1839, only five days after arriving for his third visit to see Victoria. Victoria and Albert were both born in 1819; Victoria was born on the 24th of May and Albert was born on the 26th of August.

◉⚡◉

In her journal, she said many times:

> *"Albert is so handsome and charming...a gorgeous*
> *figure, he has a fine waist and such broad*
> *shoulders; it makes my heart throb."*

◉⚡◉

Prince Albert went back to Coburg to finalize his affairs there before he moved permanently to England with Victoria. He would write Victoria letters like this one:

> *"Dearest deeply loved Victoria, I need not tell you that since we left, all my thoughts have been with you at Windsor and that your image fills my whole soul.*
>
> *Even in my dreams I never imagined that I should find so much love on earth. How that moment shines for me still when I was close to you, with your hand in mine. Those days flew by so quickly, but our separation will fly equally so."*

He tells her that his brother Ernest

> *"wishes me to say a thousand nice things to you."*

❧

The letter, in which he also tells Victoria that he had been **"*fearfully ill*"** because of rough seas on the way to Calais, is signed:

> *"With promises of unchanging love and devotion, Your ever-true Albert."*

❧

To Victoria and Albert, it seemed like months before they were to be together. Letters flew back and forth between them as preparations for a grand Royal Wedding were being prepared on a continuous basis. Everything was moving forward toward February 10, 1840.

Queen Victoria had her dress made of luxurious white satin and trimmed with blossoms of flowers in orange. The wreath that was for her headdress was also comprised of orange flower blossoms that were attached to a veil made from Honiton lace that Victoria would wear over her face. The lace alone on Victoria's dress cost 1,000 pounds. The satin for the dress was made in Spitalfields.

Queen Victoria was also to wear an armlet that had the motto for the Order of the Garter inscribed upon it. She also made sure she was going to wear the star of the Order.

All the lace used on Victoria's dress which was called Honiton lace was made in the village of Beer, located near the sea coast, and was located about ten miles from the town of Honiton. It was designed and made under the supervision of a Miss Bidney who was a native of this village, who left London, by command of Victoria just for directing all the work. It took more than two hundred employees from March to November to make all the lace that was needed.

The lace itself made up the ruffle of the wedding dress; it measured four and three-fourths yard in depth. The pattern of the lace was exquisite but tasteful in design, made expressly for this occasion which surpassed anything that had ever been designed in Brussels or England before.

Since the dressmaker was so bent on making sure Victoria had a dress that was to be unique to all other dresses, they destroyed the design of the lace, so it could never be made again.

Victoria's veil, made from the same lace, allowed for employment to more people for more than six more weeks. It measured 48" by 48". All in all, Victoria's dress was made entirely of everything from British manufacturers.

The Duchess of Kent wore white satin brocaded with silver that had three flounces of blonde. It was trimmed with silver and netting. It had a train of sky-blue velvet also lined with white satin, and it was embellished with mink. The bodice of the dress and the sleeves were trimmed with mink and silver with the blonde ruffles. She wore a headdress of feathers and diamonds.

The day of the ceremony was February 10th, 1840. It was to be held at St. Jame's in the Royal Chapel. The wedding day was a bit of disappointment because there was heavy rain falling. It did not matter however to keep the multitudes of her country from assembling and watching what they could of the wedding procession.

Buckingham Palace was in a flurry of activity getting ready to leave to go to St. Jame's.

⚜

Victoria had given Prince Albert a wedding gift of the Star and Badge of the Garter that was set in diamonds. Prince Albert gifted Victoria a beautiful brooch that was studded with a diamond and sapphire.

⚜

Victoria, her mother, and her twelve bridesmaids all gathered early for preparation for the wedding. Princess Sophia Matilda who came from Gloucester, Princess Mary, the Duchess of Cambridge, The Duchess of Gloucester, Princess Augusta of Cambridge all arrived early at the Palace and could come into Victoria's apartment.

⚜

At 12:00 noon, the bridal party started from Buckingham Palace to head toward St. Jame's, where the wedding was to be held. The procession started moving through the arch; a 21-gun salute was the announcement that Victoria was getting into her carriage. It seemed that every nook of the park at St. Jame's that lay between the palaces had been filled with people from a very early hour that morning.

⚜

It was barely daybreak with all the crowds of loyal but anxious subjects were hurrying from every part of the city trying to vie for a spot to see as much as they could of the

Royal wedding. In St. Jame's Park, in front of Buckingham Palace, the avenue that leads from the garden entrance to St. Jame's was thronged before it even reached 8:00 a.m. and the rain that fell did not cause the crowds to diminish.

࿓

Victoria was given an enthusiastic greeting by all those who could be in the presence of the Queen as she went by in her carriage.

࿓

Things were already happening at St. Jame's. Prince Albert's procession was moving into place first and was preceded by the Deputy and Lord Chamberlains, who would walk Albert to the chapel where he would remain to the right of the altar. Albert had by his side his Gentlemen of Honor, the Reigning Duke (who was his elder brother and father) and they were preceded by trumpets and drums.

࿓

Prince Albert wore his field marshal's uniform, that had large rosettes made of white satin on the shoulders. He was flushed as he entered the chapel to begin the wedding. His dignified and manly bearing, and the way he met others cordially and with such a straightforward manner of those around him, immediately won all their hearts. Many in attendance said he was perfect for Queen Victoria.

࿓

When Albert reached his chair, he walked gracefully to the

Duchess of Kent and kissed her hand. He bowed to the Archbishop of Canterbury and some of the other Dignitaries from the Church. Albert kept standing for quite a while and keep looking anxiously toward the entrance to the chapel watching for his bride.

৩৯৫৩

The Deputy and Lord Chamberlain went to where Victoria was and took up their positions as they had practiced. Victoria's bridal procession went through a series of rooms which were all very adorned and in each of them were all decorated with fashion, and each had seats for spectators. There had been 2,100 tickets issued for this wedding.

৩৯৫৩

In the wedding procession, Victoria was led by heralds of trumpeters, different officers of the household, members of the Royal Family and attendants from their house, the Chamberlains, and Lord Melbourne wearing the sword of state.

৩৯৫৩

Victoria's wedding train was carried by her twelve bridesmaids, they were followed then by the ladies of her bedchamber, her maids of honor, women of the bedchamber, then six men of arms, and men of the guard.

৩৯৫৩

The wedding was beautiful with the glittering robes of state and all the costly decorations, as they formed a display of more than anyone could imagine. The altar was beautifully decorated. The pillars that were supporting the galleries were gilt, and so was the communion table and all the railing around it.

❦

Queen Victoria and Prince Albert met, and he walked her to her seat on the right of the altar. The Archbishop advanced towards the rails, and Albert walked toward him, and the wedding started. All during the wedding, Victoria could be seen looking at Albert, who was right there standing beside her. Victoria hardly took her eyes off Albert during the entire wedding.

❦

When the wedding ceremony was over, several of the Royal Family that had occupied chairs close to the altar got up to proceed out of St. Jame's. After everyone had passed by, except for Albert and Victoria, Victoria walked quickly to the other side of the altar, where her mother was standing and kissed her. Prince Albert took Victoria's hand, and they left the chapel.

❦

Queen Victoria and Prince Albert stayed in the Royal Closet for a short time and then went to get into the carriage to go back to Buckingham's Palace.

❦

They went back to Buckingham Palace for a wedding brunch with their guests. There were confections so beautiful and tasteful that were displayed everywhere to tempt all those in attendance. A splendid wedding cake was the object of attention for everyone.

❦

After eating brunch, the bridal party left to go to Windsor being attended by the military. While traveling the road they were continually being greeted by thousands of good wishers.

❦

The baker/confectioner at Buckingham Palace designed the Wedding Cake just for the wedding of Prince Albert and Queen Victoria. It had been described as "*a cake consisting of some of the most exquisite elements of all rich things that the most expensive, beautiful cakes can be designed from*." This unique wedding cake weighed almost 300 pounds and was 9 feet in circumference. It was about fourteen inches thick. It was sitting on an elegant structure that cost more than 100 pounds.

❦

The cake was covered with the purest white sugar, and the cake topper was that of the figure of Britannia blessing the Bride and Groom that were dressed up in costumes of ancient Greece. The figures were close to one foot in height. At the feet of the Prince, there was a dog to represent fidelity; and at the feet of Victoria was a pair of turtledoves, representing the delights of marriage.

❦

There was a cupid sitting down writing in a book with the volume expanded out on his knees with the date of the wedding, with other cupids wearing emblems of the United Kingdom. On the top of the cake, there were several bouquets of Orange blossoms and Myrtle that were entwined. There were similar sprigs that had been placed loosely as presents to the wedding guests at the brunch and was placed on the table used at Brunch for the Queen of Buckingham Palace that followed the ceremonies at St. Jame's.

❦

When it came to their wedding night, the newlyweds were said to make love till dawn. For Victoria with John Conroy and her mother out of her way and out of her life, for the first time, she was a delightful person. Victoria called her wedding night, "***something blissful beyond belief***," writing,

"Never has any woman been so blessed as me."

❦

In her diaries, she said that it was such a bewildering and gratifying experience; due to Albert's excessive affection and love it gave her the feeling of such happiness and love. She went on to say that he would hold her in his arms and they would kiss each other over and over.

❦

One historian said that Victoria wanted to make love so much during their marriage that to keep their kids from interrupting their lovemaking, Albert installed some switch by their bed that would activate locks on their bedroom door.

There is one claim about Victoria that seems to be the undeniable truth. Possibly she had a hormonal balance because Victoria had such an endless and constant sexual appetite that there is no way to put it but nymphomania.

From the night of their marriage, it was Victoria that made all the advances. Poor Albert was so unnerved and appalled that he was wanted day and night by Victoria that at times he would be found cowering behind his bedroom door.

It angered Victoria because she felt it was a right of being married and she would pound on his bedroom door and scream at him in German,

"You open this door! I am the Queen!"

Face it, Albert seemed to be nothing but a very used up breeding stud. Love comes beautifully and brings two people together. It does not force one's self on the other multiple times a day, every day all day and all night long.

❧ VI ❧
THERE WERE 9

"I don't dislike babies, though I think very young ones rather disgusting."

— QUEEN VICTORIA

❦

Victoria loved the sexual side of their relationship.

❦

No matter how much she liked the physical side of their relationship, she hated the consequences. She resented the emotional and physical restrictions it put on her sex life because of the childbearing with pregnancy and all those babies just got in her way of having sex.

※

The photographs and paintings from the Castle made it look like that they were a devoted young couple that was surrounded by fair-haired and obedient children.

※

Even though their sex life was explosive, they seemed to stay locked in a power struggle. Albert kept helping with more of Victoria's workload as all the pregnancies made her step to the side.

※

It conflicted Victoria; while she admired Albert for all his talents, she was feeling resentment about being robbed of her queen's powers or, so it seemed. They could get into some terrible fights, and Albert hated Victoria's tantrums. It stuck at the back of his mind that she could have inherited George III's madness. When she would go into her fits of rage, he would reduce himself to putting notes under Victoria's door rather than talk to her.

※

Victoria hated being pregnant. With repeated pregnancies, she started feeling like a guinea pig or a rabbit.

※

She especially hated breastfeeding and thought it was disgusting. She was never a doting mother and never showed affection to any of her children.

Victoria's first child was a girl. At the time of the first birth, the firstborn could not inherit the kingdom unless it was a boy child. When the doctor delivered Victoria's first baby, the disappointment was in his voice when he said,

"Oh, my queen, it is a little princess."

Queen Victoria said to never mind because the next one would be a boy. And, as Victoria had predicted, Edward VII was born the next time.

❦

Victoria gave her account of being in labor for 12 hours and stated that she had "***suffered severely***." Albert being at her side almost the entire time. Yes, Victoria did love sex but hated the after-effects of it in the pregnancy department, that part that she called the "***shadow-side***" of marriage.

❦

At this time in history, there were no anesthetics for Victoria until she was given ether (also known as chloroform) by Dr. John Snow when she had Princess Beatrice and Prince Leopold. Victoria thought it was the best thing that had ever happened and called it "***blessed chloroform***" and the effects of the chloroform were quieting, soothing, and delightful beyond anything she could describe.

❦

When Victoria reached the number of nine children (four

boys and five girls), there was no doubt that Albert was proving himself to be an admirable companion. He was making a strong statement when it came to his contribution towards British life.

❦

Prince Albert was ambitious and intelligent, and both he and Victoria wanted and worked toward putting forward to the public the model of a happy, loving family. Albert was a protecting and nourishing supporter of his family. He felt that for the family to prosper and survive, royalty must be presented as being a close-knit, happy little family unit. To make sure they looked this way led them to have many harmonious and beautiful group family portraits made.

❦

One of the reasons they felt this was because Albert and Victoria were both children from unhappy childhoods. When their first child was born, Victoria was too busy in her role as Queen that it seemed she never had time for her newborn. While Victoria ran the country, Albert worked on bringing up the children in the way they should go.

❦

Albert was strict however and developed a punishing educational system that started right at infancy. Edward yet had decided he would never follow his father's plan of action to educate Royal children.

❦

Her children were:

Victoria, Born: November 21, 1840; married Prince Frederick William of Prussia, Death: August 5, 1901; When Victoria wrote in her diary about the birth, she said that she and Albert were disappointed because it was not a baby boy, but they were still happy the baby was healthy. They called her Vicky; her entire, long name being Victoria Adelaide Mary Louise. Vicky seemed brilliant, and Albert doted on her. She and Prince Frederick were very much in love, but it was also full of political motivation. She and Fritz had eight children, and the oldest of them became Kaiser Wilhelm II.

❧❧

Albert, Prince of Wales, Born: November 9, 1841; married Princess Alexandra of Denmark, Death: May 6, 1910; He was not like his older sister. He was not very smart, was involved with a prostitute by the name of Nellie Clifden in 1861 which turned out to be a scandalous affair that led Victoria to blame him for the death of Albert later that year. However, a match was made with him and Alexandra, and they married in 1863. They had six kids and five of them made it through infancy. Bertie as Victoria called him took several foreign tours as the heir to the throne and was praised for his abilities of diplomacy.

❧❧

Princess Alice, Born April 25, 1843; married Prince Louis of Hesse and the Rhine, Death: December 1878; Princess Alice was supportive of her mother in the capacity of her official royal duties, especially after the death of her father. She married a German prince, and Victoria was furious, horrified when she found out that Victoria was going to breastfeed her baby. Victoria was so bitter and angry that she decided to name one of her palace cows "***Princess Alice***." Alice was even more involved in the nursing side during the time of the Prussian wars and making sure there were plenty of hospital provisions in Hesse due to her efforts. Becoming weaker by her hard work and two of her seven children dying, Alice died when she was 35 years old.

Prince Alfred, Born August 6, 1844; married Marie, who was the Grand Duchess of Russia, Death July 30, 1900; He was nicknamed Affie and was a favorite of Prince Albert. He loved the nautical life and joined the Navy in 1858, his duties keeping him away when Prince Albert died. His wife occasionally caused friction in the family. His wife thought her title should be above the princesses in his family. Affie did inherit the German duchy of Saxe-Coburg from his uncle Ernest in 1893 after his naval career had ended. He was missing the ocean life and being married was getting more difficult, and then his only son died making his last year's miserable ones. Affie died about six months before Victoria in July 1900.

Princess Helena, Born May 25, 1846; married Prince Christian of Schleswig-Holstein, Death June 9, 1923; Helena who was the third daughter that they nicknamed Lenchen. She was tough and a lot like her brother Affie. She had a practical mind and loved the outdoors. When Helena married their first home was in Frogmore, near Windsor because Victoria wanted at least one child to live close to her. Helena worked hard for charity work and was the president of the Association for The Royal British Nurses. She and Christian were married 50 years in 1916.

❦

Princess Louise, Born March 18, 1848; married John Campbell, Marquis of Lorne, Death December 3, 1939; She was felt to be the prettiest of the five princesses. Louise had an artistic talent from a very early age, and when she was old enough, she went to the National Art Training School at Kensington. Louise was the first female sculptor that had a public placed statue, and it was of Queen Victoria. Louise's marriage was not always happy, and it had been suggested that John Campbell had some homosexual leanings. Louise was not able to have children. She was interested in women's rights and was probably the most forward thinking of Victoria's children.

❦

Prince Arthur, Born May 1, 1850; who wed Princess Louise of Prussia, Death January 16, 1942; Arthur was Victoria's favorite son. Even when he was a small child, it was apparent that he loved soldiering and as soon as he could he joined the army in 1866. Outside of his career in the military, Prince Arthur was a great football player. 1911-1916 he was Governor General of Canada. He had three children with wife Louise. He was 91 when he died. That made him the longest-lived son of Victoria's and Albert's by more than 20 years.

❦

Prince Leopold, Born April 7, 1853; married Princess Helen of

Waldeck-Pyrmont, Death March 28, 1884; He was the youngest son of Albert and Victoria and the first realized hemophiliac in the British Royal Family. It was most likely passed down from Victoria. Because of Victoria worrying about him, he led a restricted and confined childhood. He did rebel against his mother and went to Oxford University. Leopold led a quiet life, but he went to the United States and met Helen of Waldeck-Pyrmont who he married in 1882. His health was so terrible, and just before he turned 31, he suffered a brain hemorrhage after falling down some stairs and died. Leopold had fathered two children, Charles and Alice.

⚝

Princess Beatrice, Born April 14, 1857; married Prince Henry of Battenberg, Death October 26, 1944; She was four when her father died. After his death, Victoria clung to poor Beatrice more than she did any of her other kids. Victoria did not even want Beatrice to get married, and when she did, it was under the condition that they would live with the Queen. Being a widow before she was forty, Beatrice found herself losing two of her four children. It was Beatrice that transcribed her mother's journals after her mom died, editing out what she did not want people to see and then destroying the original journals. Beatrice was the last of Victoria's and Albert's kids to die.

⚝

As Victoria's kids grew to adulthood, each of them displayed their quirks and individual personalities. For sure, one of the significant factors that saved Britain from any foreign fights during Victoria's reign as queen seemed to be the marriages of her children.

❧

Indirectly, directly it seemed Victoria was related to every royal family that was involved in any dominant European power. Even though their father died young, it seemed all the children of Victoria turned out well.

❧ VII ❧

WHAT HAPPENED
DURING HER REIGN

"I feel sure that no girl would go to the altar if she knew all."

— QUEEN VICTORIA

❈

In the very beginning of their marital bliss, Victoria did not want Albert to have any part in the running of the government. It was 'her' government, 'her' job. It was not even six months, and on Lord Melbourne's advice "*repeatedly*," she let Albert start reviewing the dispatches, and then she gave in to Albert being present when she met with her ministers.

❈

She started giving in more and more, and it was becoming

routine to see Albert in her place, and for sure when she was pregnant the first time, Albert even got a key to the "**Secret Boxes**."

⚜

Since she had one unwanted pregnancy after the other due to having sex all the time, Victoria started depending on Albert more and more. Albert was assuming a more significant role all the time in politics.

⚜

It seemed that when Baroness Lehzen, Victoria's governess (with whom she was extremely close), finally left for Germany, it was a victory for Albert. It appeared to Albert that he was always in a battle with Victoria that included Lehzen. Victoria was so loyal to Lehzen who wanted to show she had a lot of power around the Royal household.

⚜

After Lehzen left, Albert was Victoria's private secretary, or one might call him her "**permanent minister**." Albert was very diligent in his duties and refused to let the obstacles that the ministers tried to throw at him get in his way. By managing Victoria's properties, he was able to increase her value and income.

⚜

In 1845, Charles Greville, Royal Affairs observer said,

"It is pretty obvious she has a title, but he is running the Sovereign. Albert is the King."

꧁꧂

Victoria decided she was not so enthusiastic about the role of governing.

꧁꧂

Prince Albert got along well with Prime Minister Peel, and they worked out a compromise regarding the bedchamber issue after the Prime Minister Melbourne government was over once the general election had been held in 1841.

꧁꧂

Victoria's first interview with Peel went better than she had expected as it had been eased by Melbourne's prepping Peel before the meeting.

꧁꧂

Melbourne had told Peel that Victoria was not a conceited person, she realized there are a lot of things that she may not understand, and all she wants is for you to explain them to her in simple terms. She does not like a long drawn out explanation, but something short and to the point.

꧁꧂

Albert's influence and power were beginning to show outwardly when he had more royal homes built. He had Balmoral Castle made in Scotland and the Osborne House on the Isle of Wight. Albert was beginning to teach Victoria that life was not all about parties and fun all the time and she began to despise London. It helped when he got her to agree with him to buy both properties and the designing of their new homes that were built between 1845-1855.

❈

Victoria loved Osborne and called it "***their island home***" and would go there frequently. But, she was the happiest at Balmoral. Victoria grew to like the life of the Highlanders; it was a simpler life. She also came to realize there was a small stream of Scottish blood flowing through her veins.

❈

If the sermons were short, she started to like the Scottish religious services too. She told her prime minister, William Gladstone,

"I am not much of a true Episcopalian."

❈

She had grown comfortable being consoled by Reverend Macleod and delighted with the everyday speech of one John Brown who was a Highland servant, who worked for Prince Albert and eventually became her assistant.

❈

By Albert and Victoria withdrawing to the Isle of Wight and Scotland so much it bore the fact that there was a new type of British Monarchy in town. By searching for intimacy and privacy, they had learned to adapt to a way of life that was much like that of the middle-class subjects even if on a more grand scale.

⚜

Albert's interests held to scientific and intellectual issues while Victoria's tastes were reading Charles Dickens, the waxwork shows, and the circus.

⚜

Albert and Victoria both were different than the middle class in their preferences for nudes in sculpture and painting. There was no way Victoria was the prude she was made out to be. She also did not approve of dull Sundays either, and she made it well known.

⚜

Even with Victoria mingling among the poor of the Scottish while at Balmoral, it did little to raise her ability to see what was right in front of her. In 1846 Albert and Victoria supported to repeal the Corn Laws (it protected the legislation that would keep British grain prices fraudulently high) to relieve distress for Ireland who was stricken by famine. It did not seem to matter though to Albert and Victoria as they still were more involved and interested with building Osborne house and new foreign policy than the tragedy taking place in Ireland. How they could turn their backs on the hungry in their own country and keep building more homes and palaces makes one wonder. Once again, history seems to repeat itself.

⚜

It seemed like Victoria had no idea what was happening in her back door. Many of her subjects were living in *"misery,"* and Victoria would not even bring it up, let alone think about it.

⚜

For Prince Albert and Queen Victoria, the real highlight of their reign was to come in 1851 when the Great Exhibition opened. Albert worked hard at organizing the tradeshow that was '*international*' and became a Victorian Age symbol. It was housed in the Crystal Palace which was an architectural marvel itself, a fabulous greenhouse – a glass building that had been built in Hyde Park. The Exhibition would display Britain's technological achievements and its wealth to the world.

⚜

For Victoria, this success at the Crystal Palace for the Great Exhibition only provided more evidence of the genius of her husband. She felt so proud of what her beloved Albert's great mind had designed and made come into being. The profits from this Exhibition would fund what would one day become the complex of museums and complex of colleges in South Kensington.

⚜

Albert was also given credit for showing Victoria how crucial it was not to take party sides. He had seen the dangers in the Whig partisanship that Victoria had openly demonstrated before they got married. Albert realized that a monarch should maintain a sense of balance no matter what.

When it came to Albert's actions, for instance, his appearance up in the gallery at the House of Commons when Peel gave a speech the very first day about the Corn Laws where he showed his support for Peel and revealed which side he stood for, showed where Albert stood.

It was noted in 1846 that: The Prince is very firmly a Conservative with his politics and his influence with Queen Victoria is over-ruling; through him, she is becoming attached to Conservative ideas that she would hardly endure the idea of the opposite Party as her ministers.

Albert knew the queen had an active and vital role in British politics. But, the fluidness of the political airs that were operating at the time the prince lived made his active role possible.

When the Corn Laws (1846) were repealed, there was a period, that did not end until 1868 after the election, when it seemed politics started to consist of alliances even if they were temporary between small splinter factions. There was not a single group that was able to feel it could guarantee it held long time control over the House of Commons: it seemed the golden age of the private members, which was a condition that rendered an active intervention politically by the queen not only possible but at times it had to happen.

To help compose the coalitions, a role opened for a "***cabinet maker***" position.

Do not let her importance be overemphasized; as Victoria would have never admitted to it, but her role, was always secondary.

Albert had made up his mind that his intelligence was not going to be disregarded and that Victoria would not become a figure that would nod her head in agreement or denial with whatever her Prime Minister pleased.

Because of this, there was a clash with Lord Palmerston who was the foreign secretary who had been in high offices since before Victoria was even born. Albert never trusted Palmerston and had disapproved of the way he handled issues. He felt that Palmerston's policies were weak and had always disagreed with the way he translated the constitution.

Victoria told Palmerston in 1850 if she put her name on a sanction, that no one better not modify or alter it in any way. It didn't matter, Palmerston forged ahead and followed policies that both Victoria and Albert had disapproved. He even encouraged movements nationally that could cause the Austrian Empire to dismember.

⚜

The straw that broke the camel's back was when Palmerston announced his approval of Napoleon III without saying anything to the queen. The prime minister who was Lord John Russell at the time removed Palmerston from office.

⚜

Within a very few months, Palmerston who was popular with the people found himself back in office, but as home secretary. He then served two terms as Prime Minister.

⚜

Oddly enough, after Albert had died, Victoria changed her mind about Palmerston. It seemed his conservative policies and him being insistent that Britain should receive what was due Britain on the world stage of affairs. It went right along with what Victoria believed.

⚜

It was the eve of the Crimean War (1854-1856) when Victoria and Albert became unpopular. Albert without foundation was suspected of trying to sway the British government to bend in favor for the Russian cause.

⚜

Victoria became involved with the committees of the ladies

to organize relief for wounded soldiers and worked to support the efforts of Florence Nightingale. Victoria visited with the crippled soldiers who were in the hospitals and started the Victoria Cross that was to be given for gallantry.

࿇

After Albert died, it was the end of the '***Albertine monarchy***.' It did not matter, Albert's influence on Victoria was everlasting. One-handedly Albert had been able to change her political sympathies and her personal habits. He trained her in organized ways to conduct business, how to work hard, and what was expected of Royal intervention and establishing a private intelligence (royal) secret service abroad. Albert had put his stamp on the British Monarchy for the good.

✿ VIII ✿

LOVES FLAME
BURNS OUT

"We are not interested in the possibilities of defeat.
They do not exist."

— QUEEN VICTORIA

✿

The light is soft in the Blue Room of Windsor. Albert is lying
in his bed with ample pillows plumped all around him. This
42-year-old prince had been sick for over four weeks. His
breathing is labored and slow; his skin is as white as a sheet
with his hair soaked in sweat.

✿

Kneeling next to him on her knees on the floor beside his
bed, Victoria is trembling. She is holding on to his limp hand

and knows for sure he has to be dying. Five of their children filled with fear is standing close by them. Awkwardly there are doctors, ministers, and different ladies in waiting standing around.

❧

His illness started out at the beginning of November, maybe even in the middle. You know how illness can creep up on you and it is hard to define the exact day that it all started. Albert's symptoms at first were arm and leg pain, he had terrible insomnia, and he had no appetite.

❧

Details from the palace must have been gossip about the prince's illness. The details as the public got them were imprecise and very vague. In the palace, however, the Royals felt that Albert had some "*gastric*" or what they called then "*low*" fever, which was both words used for typhoid fever.

❧

Typhoid fever was usually contracted when one drank water infected with the Salmonella Typhi bacteria. We must bear in mind this was the time before antibiotics and IV fluids, so a bout of Typhoid could last 21 to 30 days. You could not be sure it would end with you living or dying. If you lived, it would be with a long recovery as you would be so emancipated. The symptoms were bloody diarrhea, stomach pain, and fever.

❧

The last week of Albert's life, he became more dehydrated and disoriented. He was having difficulty breathing and had begun coughing a lot. Press reports were contradicting themselves on Albert's condition. Rumors were spreading.

❦

Albert had a long-lasting influence on Victoria. He had been able to change her political sympathies and personal habits. The British monarchy had seemed to change.

❦

It had been several weeks before Albert died when he had told Victoria about how depressed he felt and that he just wanted to die. He said to her that he did not feel like clinging to life and that if he only knew that all those he loved would be taken care of, it would be easy for him to die the next day. He went on to say that if he was sure he had a terrible, severe illness, he would give up immediately. He could not struggle anymore as he had no tenacity.

❦

It does not matter; Victoria cannot see anyone but Albert, the love of her life. It is nearing 11:00 p.m. As he is slipping away, Victoria mutters,

"Oh, this death, I know it."

When he died, Victoria screamed so loudly that it felt that the walls of the castle were going to collapse around everyone.

History tells us for over a century that Albert probably died from typhoid fever. In recent years, doctors and pathologists have been rethinking and arguing it was more than typhoid.

❦

It seems that it was overlooked at the time that he had been experiencing lengthy medical issues of intestinal obstructions, diarrhea, intermittent abdominal cramps, anorexia, rheumatic joint problems, and fatigue.

❦

There have been some doctors who had considered forms of abdominal cancer (we must remember his mother did die of stomach cancer when she was 30). Other physicians argue that Albert could have had ulcerative colitis or Crohn's disease that was accompanied by a perforated bowel running into sepsis and then death. We will never know the real reason for his death, but poor Albert did suffer for sure, and he did die before his time.

❦

When Albert died, Victoria became unable to function. With such a miserable childhood, Albert completely transformed her life. He was gorgeous; he loved her like no one else ever had, he was so passionate in the bedroom and gave her excellent advice regarding her government. Albert was not just her husband, but her lover as well. He was her everything.

❦

When she lost all the things that Albert was to her at 42 years of age, she had to feel as if every light in the world had gone out. Victoria did not know how she could go on, how she could put one foot in front of the other as her grief was so heavy.

༺⚜༻

Victoria went into a deep, deep depression. It was a depression of yearning, longing, despair, and even a longing at night to die that remained for the first three years after he died. When she started to climb out from under the depression, she stayed in mourning and even in a semi-retirement.

༺⚜༻

Victoria's oldest son Bertie, who later came to be known as Edward VII, was terrible. Victoria considered him to be disappointment from the beginning.

༺⚜༻

Like other princes, his education up to a point at home in the castle by a tutor. Bertie was terrible with his lessons and Albert, and Victoria seriously considered him challenged. Victoria even said of her son that he was in no way handsome because he had such a narrow head, no chin, and large features. The poor boy, not even one his mother could seem to love.

༺⚜༻

Bertie was 19, and he started training in the army in Ireland, and someone smuggled a prostitute in his bed. The story, of course, reached home, and Albert was devastated. He wrote Bertie a long, very emotional letter about the situation.

ठ✿ठ

Albert even went to Cambridge to visit Bertie, and they went for a long walk in the rain. When Albert got back to Windsor, he was very sick, and this was the beginning of the end for Albert.

ठ✿ठ

Victoria held a hard grudge, and she blamed Bertie for Albert's death. She could hardly look at him.

ठ✿ठ

She did not feel like being at ceremonial functions that they expected the Queen to oversee. Victoria started to withdraw to Osborne and Balmoral for months at a time out of every year no matter if it was inconvenient and caused a considerable strain for the ministers in parliament. After they allowed time for sympathy and respect for Victoria's grieving, her people started to grow impatient when their Queen was always absent. It did not matter to Victoria. She was still depressed and still mourning her Albert.

ठ✿ठ

Victoria just refused to carry out her duties as Queen for about three years. But then Victoria determined to be an effective politician even after Albert's death and try her best to do as he would have wanted her to perform.

Victoria continued to blame her son, the Prince of Wales, for Albert's death. Victoria was angry at the time, and she did not mind telling the Prince of Wales over and over many times about her loneliness caused by him and refused him any responsibilities.

She could barely stand to look at him. It seemed this deepening breach was never totally healed between them. As time passed, Victoria started being envious of the prince and princess of Wales, and it was becoming very evident. Victoria seemed to be having issues with realizing that she was still popular with the people too.

I am sure she was criticized for the fact that she spent years mourning for Albert and she will always be remembered in history for that period of her life. In the end, however, Victoria had more than one love story, but Albert was still her one true love that no other could ever surpass.

In today's world, it seems we live in a throwaway society. There are drive-through funeral homes for those who do not have time to even get out of their cars and walk inside the funeral home to extend their sympathies. We live in a time when death happens, and the mourning is lost as everyone goes back to their work week and forgets about the emptiness for those left behind. Life is too busy.

❦

This writer can tell you for sure that grief has no timetable and understands and sympathizes with Victoria. There is no set time for one to say you should get over your grief. And such it was for Victoria. Many make fun of her for the fact that she never got over her husband Albert, her one great love.

❦

Today, women may not wear black for the rest of their lives, but I know many, many women and men who have lost the love of their lives, and never remarry, because, in their heart of hearts, no one can ever take the place of "*their Albert*."

IX

SHE DEFIES DEATH

"We poor creatures are born for man's pleasure and amusement and destined to go through endless sufferings and trials."

— QUEEN VICTORIA

You cannot please all the people all the time is for sure. During Queen Victoria's reign, her life was attempted to be cut short by approximately seven different people during her reign as queen. Some tried for the notoriety, some because they were just plain crazy, but none who truly wanted to kill her.

JUNE 10TH, 1840 - EDWARD OXFORD

ও৫ও

I t was close to 6:00 p.m. when Victoria and Albert were leaving their garden gate from Buckingham Palace in their German Carriage on their way to see Victoria's mother, the Duchess of Kent. As their carriage turned the corner and progressed along Constitution-Hill, there was a young man who shot at them. He had been standing with his back against the fence. At first, the carriage started to pause, but Albert hurried it along. Spectators grabbed the shooter and gave him to the City Police. It was later realized that the subject was 18 years old and had fired two different pistols at the carriage. When he was tried in court, and there could be no balls found that came from the pistols, he was found guilty on the grounds of insanity, and if Victoria was the Queen, he would be held in prison.

MAY 30TH, 1842 – JOHN FRANCIS

⊰⊱

The second time someone attempted to take Victoria's life was close to be the same as it was two years prior. They had gone out for an evening carriage ride about 6:00 p.m. again and were coming back to the palace in their open carriage when a John Francis tried to take a shot into their ride. The police constable rushed him to try to knock his pistol from his hand. As the constable grabbed the pistol, it fired, but it did not harm the Queen or Albert.

⊰⊱

John Francis was bound over for trial where he was found guilty and that he was to be hanged by his neck till dead; then his head was to be cut from his body, his body then divided into four complete quarters and disposed of as the Queen desired.

The Queen took mercy on him and had him sent to Australia where he was sentenced to a life of hard labor.

JULY 3RD, 1842 – JOHN WILLIAM BEAN

❦

P rince Albert and Queen Victoria while traveling to the Chapel Royal by carriage when a humpbacked boy in a long coat shoved his way up to the front of the crowd that was standing, and he pulled a pistol. Near him was a 16-year-old Charles Dassett who grabbed Beans wrist. Dassett took Bean over to two police officers who were walking on the other side of the street. Dassett showed them that Bean had been attempting to shoot at the Queen. They just laughed at Dassett and told him to release Bean.

❦

Then Dassett, the good Samaritan was taken to the police station for being caught with a pistol in his hand in Green Park. He told them his story about the humpback boy. They called in witnesses, and the two police officers were suspended from duty that had not taken Dassett seriously.

Dassett was taken into custody. Bean said that he did not want to hurt the Queen, but he just wanted to be arrested. He said all he had in the gun was some paper and powder. He went on to state that he had been waiting for three days for a chance and when he did he pointed the gun at the ground. He was found guilty and imprisoned at Newgate for 18 months.

MAY 19TH, 1849 – WILLIAM
HAMILTON

❧❦❧

Again, the Royal Carriage was involved in an incident while proceeding down Constitution Hill when someone fired at it. The carriage was heading towards Buckingham. The pistol fire came from Green-Park. Victoria was by herself and the time was about 5:50 p.m. She was not harmed.

❧❦❧

The suspect was apprehended quickly by the police and taken to the Palace then to the police station. He was approximately 22 years old, a bricklayer, an orphan and he was Irish.

❧❦❧

He was sent for "***transportation beyond the seas***" to last for seven years.

JUNE 27TH, 1850 – ROBERT PATE

৩৯৩

A t 6:20 p.m. Victoria and three of her children along with her lady in waiting, Viscountess Jocelyn, were leaving Piccadilly from Cambridge House to go back to Buckingham Palace. When the carriage entered through the gates of the Palace grounds, a man dressed nicely ran out from nowhere and hit Victoria with a hard blow to her head with his cane. Some onlookers ran forward and grabbed the man as if they, themselves were going to hang him right then. Sergeant Silver took the man to the police station.

৩৯৩

The stick that he used was not any thicker than a goose quill and was about two foot in length. It only weighed three ounces.

৩৯৩

He was examined many times by doctors to try and reach the decision if he were sane. He stayed in prison until time for trial. There were many witnesses called that vowed that he was not a man of sound mind. Even though at the trial he was found to be of unsound mind, it was felt he knew right from wrong and found guilty and was transported for seven years.

FEBRUARY 29TH, 1872 – ARTHUR O'CONNOR

❦

A young boy of eighteen or nineteen ran into Buckingham Garden when the Queen entered in her carriage. He followed her carriage to the door, a short distance, pointed a pistol a foot from Victoria's head. Victoria bowed her head, and someone captured the boy. The gun was not loaded. The boy had a Fenian document in his hand, and it is thought he was going to try and force her to sign it. The Queen was not frightened and had Colonel Hardinge to present to Parliament immediately so that false rumors would not be spread.

❦

He was a clerk at an oil and color manufacturer and lived with his mother and father. He was judged guilty and given a sentence to one year in prison and beaten with twenty strokes by a birch rod.

MARCH 2ND, 1882 – RODERICK MCLEAN

꧁꧂

Victoria left Buckingham Palace at 4:00 p.m. to take her carriage to Paddington Station to catch her train to Windsor. There was hail falling, but it did not matter because crowds still gathered on the route to cheer and wave at the Queen when the train pulled out from the station. As the train got to Windsor station and Victoria was getting into her carriage, there was a man in the station who fired at Victoria. The police grabbed him and took him to the police station. McLean was found to be a lunatic and acquitted on the grounds of insanity.

X

RUMORS OF OTHER LOVES

"Affairs go on, and all will take some shape or other, but it keeps one in hot water all the time."

— QUEEN VICTORIA

To some, it appeared that the queen at age 50 even though still grieving over Albert who had died seven years prior, had lost her ever-loving mind. It was brought up because she became so close to the rough-spoken ghillie who was Scottish that had worked at their Balmoral estate. It would be one, John Brown.

❧

John was seven years younger than Victoria, and anywhere you saw Victoria, you saw John. He even stood guard when she was in her room at Windsor Castle. He would relay messages and bar entry to those who thought they were the highest people of the kingdom.

༺❀༻

John was found to be drunk most of the time, and he soon made Victoria his favorite drinking partner. It is the reason why everyone felt he and Victoria were lovers. The Royal household called him the "*Queen's Stallion*."

༺❀༻

When Brown was 21 years old, he started working as a servant outdoors at Balmoral when Prince Albert first decided in 1848 to lease the castle. Even though happily married to Albert she took a shine to Brown, but then her entire world dropped from her when Albert died. After she went into her deep depression, it was noticed that toward the end of 1864 the one thing that seemed to make her happy was taking rides in the pony cart with Brown.

༺❀༻

She soon had John Brown moved to England. As soon as he arrived, he was Victoria's constant companion; he would bring in her morning mail and stay while she worked through it. He would take her for rides and act as her gatekeeper.

༺❀༻

John had a great sense of humor, but he came across as pompous with courtiers and unlike everyone else was not afraid of Victoria. Queen Victoria told Uncle Leopold who was King of Belgium, that John Brown was intelligent and not like the ordinary servant.

※※※

Victoria would have him call different members of the household to her room which he did in such a language that it was regarded to be ill-mannered.

※※※

When Albert had been dead for four years, Victoria took her children to his mausoleum at Frogmore. Who else, but Brown went with them.

※※※

Victoria went so far as to hire John Brown's brother, Archie for a valet to her son who was the hemophiliac, Prince Leopold, even though Leopold could not stand John Brown or Archie.

※※※

And of course, there was talk that with John Brown and Victoria had three children together. One child was sent to live in New York, and two of them sent to live in Paris. They were sent 275 pounds quarterly as this was documented in the Palace records. It was believed that Victoria did divulge these secrets to her daughter very late in her life. A good reason for her daughter to go through all her diaries and get rid of some of the documentation and burn it so it would never see the light of day.

Leopold told others that John Brown was not kind to him as he would hit Leopold on the face with spoons for fun.

When Victoria would make a public appearance which was extremely rare, it scandalized the politicians as she was always dragging Brown along. Lord Stanley, the Foreign Secretary, said,

> *"Victoria parades John Brown all over London behind her coach, him wearing his Highland dress, and every wife in the street knows him."*

Her older daughter Vicky who corresponded much with Victoria felt that in her mother's early years of mourning Albert there was no way she would be sexually intimate with Brown.

However, ten years later, she had a new doctor, James Reid that was taken aback by the physical intimacy and ease that he saw between Brown and the Queen. When Victoria sprained her knee, John carried her where ever she wanted to go.

It was March 1883 when John went on a walk with Victoria

even though he was sick with a bad cold. When the next day came, he had a fever and was dead within 48 hours. John Brown was 56.

⚜

Victoria was beside herself again. She gave instructions that if and when she died to make sure she be buried with John Brown's mother's plain gold wedding band and a picture of John Brown in her hands. To cover the ring and the picture of Brown she was holding in her hand, Dr. Reid placed a bunch of flowers in her hands to cover them both to prevent further gossip.

⚜

Dr. Reid was one of the very few people who knew the full story about Victoria's relationship with John Brown.

⚜

There was found in a journal of the wife of the Queen's personal secretary and a sister to Victoria's Scottish chaplain. When the Chaplain was on his deathbed, he told his sister that it was he that had married John Brown and Victoria and he had always wished he had not.

⚜

Now, is this true? This writer feels it would almost have to be as why would someone waste their time writing down a story that her brother gave her on his deathbed when she could be writing other words uttered by him. It is doubtful she would have put words in his mouth as this was a private journal and not found for years.

☙❧

Benjamin Disraeli had been appointed as Prime Minister in 1868. Victoria was always buying him gifts, and he was sending thank you notes which were very seductive in nature.

☙❧

Age did not matter to Victoria. When she was named the Empress of India at age 68, she was given an Indian servant by the name of Abdul Karim who was very young to come to the palace to serve her Indian guests. He taught her about his country and his culture and even his native language of Hindu. She called him her Munshi.

☙❧

When he joined the household, he was waiting tables as a servant, but she quickly elevated him to her "**_Indian Secretary_**."

☙❧

Victoria then GAVE Abdul three homes; a bungalow for the Isle of Wight, a cottage house at Windsor, and a beautiful home at Balmoral and what did he do but fill them all with his relatives that did not have a dime to their names and the British were footing the bills.

☙❧

Victoria secured land for Abdul back in Agra because she knew when she went to her grave that there was no telling what her family would do to him and Victoria felt for sure that it would be terrible in the way they treated him.

❦

When Abdul and his family were chased from their residences, they burned all the 300 letters between Abdul and Victoria. There was one thing that escaped, and that was a journal kept by Abdul about his life with Victoria from which most of the story about their life together comes about.

❦

Abdul, at age 46, in 1909, eight years after Queen Victoria, died at his home in Agra with the cause of death unknown.

❦ XI ❧
VICTORIA'S REIGN, DEATH, LEGACY

"Bring me a cup of tea and the 'Times.'"

— QUEEN VICTORIA

❦❧

Queen Victoria was about to begin her Diamond Jubilee; she had survived sixty years on the throne.

❦❧

Victoria who was less than five-foot-tall still gave her name to the "***Victorian Age***" and developed an empire that had 387 million subjects and 40 million square kilometers.

❦❧

The Victorian age could be summed up as an era of strait-laced morality, extreme sexual repression (whether Victoria repressed her sexuality or not!), and invincible ignorance.

❧

Victoria never allowed her government to develop any legislation that was against lesbianism, not that she approved of it. Victoria did not think that lesbianism was physically possible.

❧

Victoria always liked to go to Osborn House for Christmas after she became a widow. It was in 1901, she did the same and headed for the Isle of Wight.

❧

It was in early January, she started feeling unwell and weak, and when it reached the middle of the month, she was dazed, confused, and drowsy.

❧

January 22, 1901, Queen Victoria died at 81 years old from a stroke.

❧

Victoria had been explicit in her instructions regarding her funeral and had arranged it in 1897, four years prior. She wanted her funeral to be held like that of a soldier's daughter who was the head of an army.

She wanted her mourning dress that was usually black to now be white. She also asked that she be dressed in her wedding veil which had once been white.

She lay in state for two days, and her funeral was February 2, 1901. She was buried next to the true love of her life, Prince Albert in the Frogmore Mausoleum in Windsor Park.

Victoria wrote all the time; her biographies say she wrote 2500 words a day starting in 1832 to almost up to the day of her death. She was meticulous with her diaries.

After Victoria's death, it was Beatrice, her youngest, that was appointed to edit the diaries and then burned the originals.

Victoria was what you might call "*stout*," but in today's time, people would call it "*obese*." As a widow, her popularity went down, but she seemed to regain it during the 1880s and 1890s.

While Victoria reigned, she maintained the establishment of constitutional monarchy for Britain. The voting system reformed, and this increased the powers of the Queen, House of Lords, and the House of Commons.

⚜

Under this monarchy, the Queen still held the right to encourage, warn and be consulted.

⚜

Victoria had two daughters and her youngest son that had Hemophilia B which was also passed along to some of the grandchildren as well. What is strange about this? Never before had it shown up in any of the Royal Family nor the Duchess of Kent's family.

⚜

However, there is a definite question that Victoria may have been the child of John Conroy and he passed the hemophilia gene on to Victoria to carry and bequeath. We will most likely ever know the truth about this story I am sure.

⚜

Victoria often wondered about John Conroy and her mother's relationship as she had caught them in compromising situations in the past.

⚜

With the Victorian era, strong family values were popular, and it tended to the middle class. It also widened the gap between the poor and the middle class.

At the time of Victoria's death, she had 37 great-grandchildren. This author somehow wonders what kind of grandmother she was with her grandchildren.

Even though Victoria could not stand her son Bertie, he never did break off relations with Victoria. When Victoria did die, he became the King of England at the age of 59, and as history tells us, he did an excellent job.

Bertie was able to modernize the monarchy his mother left behind, which many felt was the real reason that Britain made it through World War I when so many other countries did not. Who knows, maybe Victoria wasn't so bad a mum after all!

❧ XII ☙
STRENGTHS

❈

- She listened well to Prime Minister Melbourne and learned much from him. She never went into her role as Queen feeling she knew everything about government and how it worked. (This holds true for any job or position we take on today. We should know as much as possible about it before we take it on to lessen our likelihood of failure.)
- She appeared to have a tough exterior to the some, but to some, she was found to be lenient. Such as the men found guilty who tried to kill her.
- She believed strongly in her country and was a true patriot. (What are we if we are not proud of our country? If we cannot be proud of our country, then maybe we should move from the country in which we live.)

- She was never afraid to speak what was on her mind and never worried about what others were saying about her. She lived life on her own terms. It is to be respected especially in someone who is in public office for as long as Victoria. (You do not have to speak your mind in hurtful words, but to speak the truth about your opinion is very important.)
- Her duty to herself and history to journal 2500 words a day for almost her entire life from age thirteen till death. (Journaling your life may not seem important, however, it is even if for your family.)

❧ XIII ☙
WEAKNESSES

❧❦❧

- She was a terrible mother for the fact she could show no affection to her children even though it was probably a product of her terrible childhood with her mother.
- Her mind was more on sex than it was on more pressing issues that should have concerned her, and this was probably due to a hormonal imbalance.
- She seemed never to feel that she could be without a man. After Albert, she went far below her class to find male companionship. She did not care what others thought.
- She let her husband Albert take over her Queen duties once she started having children; not because she doted or wanted to take care of them.

❦ XIV ❦

RECOMMENDED READS

❦

- Victoria The Queen by Julia Baird. This book is new and comes in with a four-star review. The biographer went to great lengths to dig the dirt on Queen Victoria. The Archive Society did not want her to leave a big portion in the book, however, she left it in the book anyway. This book bears reading.
- Queen Victoria Edition 1 by Walter L. Arnstein. This book comes away with a four-star review.
- Victoria & Abdul by Shrabani Basu: The True Story of the Queen's Closest Confidant and this book comes away with a 3.5-star review.
- John Brown: Queen Victoria's Highland Servant by Raymond Lamont Brown this will probably only be found as a used book.

✸ XV ✸
CONCLUSION

❧

Queen Victoria shall always be remembered in history. Her life and time changed the way history evolved, not just in England, but around the world.

❧

She was raised in a world of prestige and unlimited wealth; never having to worry about anything that her heart desired. However, she did learn that money could not buy life nor keep death at bay when it came to her sweet Albert.

❧

Yes, it is odd that she took up with so many men after being married to Albert who she declared her love for and wore mourning clothes for the rest of her life. But, one must remember that if it was true and she was a nymphomaniac, then she was only finding men to keep her sexual desires at bay even in her elderly years.

🐚

Yes, my young friends, even the elderly still have a feeling of lust and desire if their health is good.

🐚

It is sad that she never really knew the love of her mother and that losing her "*father*" while so young, she never remembered his affections. It was too late when she realized that deep down her mother did indeed love her because while her mother was being influenced by John Conley, her mother was another person and did not put her child first.

🐚

It seems that because she never was the recipient of real love and affection of her mother and was raised alone, it probably made it more difficult for her to be affectionate with her children; even if she said it was because they got in the way of sex.

🐚

What matters when all is said and done is that she will go down in history as being one of the most memorable queens of England and that she was a strong force in shaping the destiny of the entire world.

YOUR FREE EBOOK!

As a way of saying thank you for reading our book, we're offering you a free copy of the below eBook.

Happy Reading!

36711127R00068